Nature's RECORD-BREAKERS

Natural Disasters

Nature's RECORD-BREAKERS

Natural Disasters

Written by Joyce E. Newson

Illustrated by Matteo Chesi, Pier Luigi Faleschini, Antonio Meschini, Andrea Morandi, Alessandro Cantucci, and Ivan Stalio

Gareth Stevens Publishing
A WORLD ALMANAC EDUCATION GROUP COMPANY

Please visit our web site at: www.garethstevens.com
For a free color catalog describing Gareth Stevens Publishing's
list of high-quality books and multimedia programs,
call 1-800-542-2595 or fax your request to (414) 332-3567.

Library of Congress Cataloging-in-Publication Data

Newson, Joyce E.
    Natural disasters / written by Joyce E. Newson; illustrated by Matteo Chesi ... [et al.].
        p. cm. — (Nature's record-breakers)
    Includes bibliographical references and index.
    Summary: Discusses various types of natural disasters, including earthquakes, volcanoes,
tornadoes, hurricanes, fires, floods, droughts, famine, epidemics, and plagues.
    ISBN 0-8368-2906-9 (lib. bdg.)
    1. Natural disasters—Juvenile literature. [1. Natural disasters.] I. Chesi, Matteo, ill.
II. Title. III. Series.
  GB5019.N49   2002
  363.34—dc21   2001049916

This edition first published in 2002 by
Gareth Stevens Publishing
A World Almanac Education Group Company
330 West Olive Street, Suite 100
Milwaukee, Wisconsin 53212 USA

Original edition © 1999 by McRae Books Srl. First published in 1999 as *Natural Disasters,* with
the series title *Blockbusters!,* by McRae Books Srl., via de' Rustici 5, Florence, Italy. This edition
© 2002 by Gareth Stevens, Inc. Additional end matter © 2002 by Gareth Stevens, Inc.

Translated from Italian by Christina Longman
Designer: Marco Nardi
Layout: Ornella Fassio and Adriano Nardi
Gareth Stevens editors: Monica Rausch
Gareth Stevens designer: Scott M. Krall

Printed in the United States of America

1 2 3 4 5 6 7 8 9 06 05 04 03 02

Contents

Words that appear in the glossary are printed in **boldface** type
the first time they occur in the text.

Q. WHAT CAUSES AN EARTHQUAKE?

A. Earthquakes occur when the outermost layer of Earth, called the crust, shifts or moves. The crust is made up of enormous plates that fit together like puzzle pieces. These plates are constantly moving and shifting. When two plates run into each other or slide past each other, pressure builds along the edges of the plates. This pressure causes rocks along the edges to bend, then break. When the rocks break, they shake the ground. The shakes start deep below Earth's surface and spread out in waves, called seismic waves. The point on Earth's surface directly above where the rock begins to break is called the epicenter.

Q. IS IT POSSIBLE TO PREDICT AN EARTHQUAKE?

A. Earthquake experts, called seismologists, know that most earthquakes occur where plates meet, but scientists cannot predict exactly when earthquakes will occur or how strong they will be.

➤ The worst place to be during an earthquake is near its epicenter. The ground shakes the most at this spot.

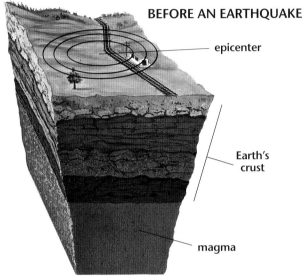

BEFORE AN EARTHQUAKE

epicenter

Earth's crust

magma

The dangers caused by earthquakes continue even after the quake is over. Earthquakes often cause landslides, avalanches, and floods. Fires can also start when power lines are damaged.

AFTER AN EARTHQUAKE

ground fault

buildings destroyed by the earthquake

movement of the plates

▲ Children who live in places often hit by earthquakes are taught what to do in case of a quake. They find shelter beneath desks or archways to protect themselves from falling objects.

➤ About 80 percent of the world's major earthquakes occur in the "ring of fire," an area along plate edges in and near the Pacific Ocean. This area is also scattered with volcanoes.

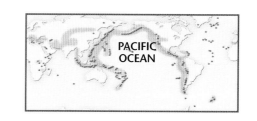

PACIFIC OCEAN

➤ Some people believe animals can sense when an earthquake is going to hit. Before the Messina-Reggio earthquake of 1908, many dogs in the area began to howl.

The most devastating earthquake ever was the quake that shook Egypt and Syria in 1201. More than one million people died as a result of the quake. This quake took the most lives of any other natural disaster in recorded history.

Fascinating Fact

The Richter Scale is the most commonly used scale for measuring the strength of earthquakes. This scale starts with a measurement of 1. An earthquake of 1 produces shakes so slight they can only be sensed by a seismograph, a machine that measures the strength and direction of seismic waves. An earthquake of 9 on the Richter Scale is **catastrophic**. The scale has no upper limit, but there are no records of an earthquake measuring more than 9. The earthquake that hit Turkey in 1999 and killed more than 14,000 measured 7.4 on the scale.

Rescue teams go to work after an earthquake.

Volcanoes

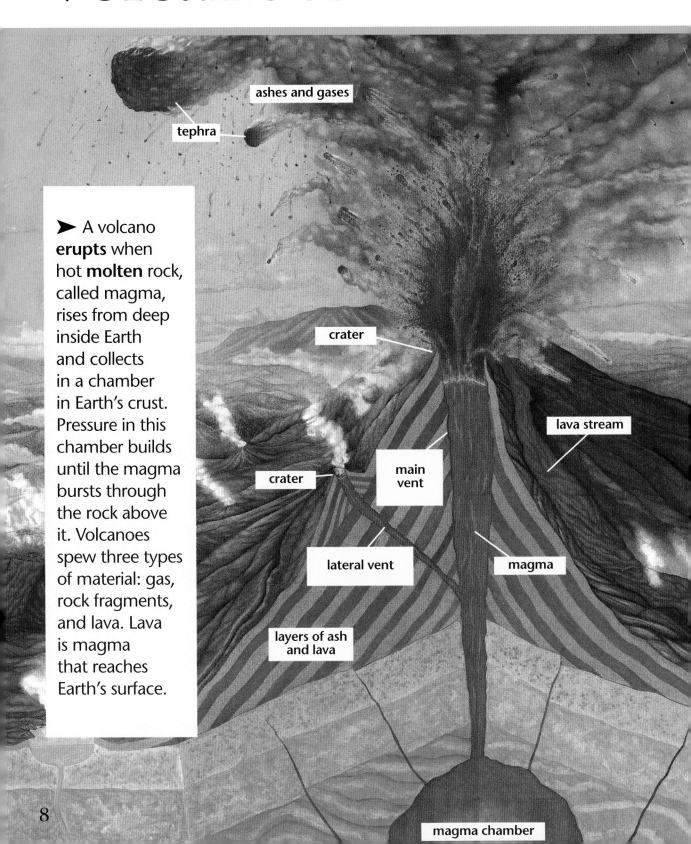

ashes and gases

tephra

> ➤ A volcano **erupts** when hot **molten** rock, called magma, rises from deep inside Earth and collects in a chamber in Earth's crust. Pressure in this chamber builds until the magma bursts through the rock above it. Volcanoes spew three types of material: gas, rock fragments, and lava. Lava is magma that reaches Earth's surface.

crater

lava stream

crater

main vent

lateral vent

magma

layers of ash and lava

magma chamber

Volcanoes exist on several other planets in the Solar System, including Mars and Venus. Volcanoes are also present on Io, one of Jupiter's moons.

▼ Mount Vesuvius in Italy is one of the most studied volcanoes. Its eruption in A.D. 79 was the first volcanic eruption recorded in great detail. The eruption buried the Roman cities of Pompeii and Herculaneum in ash. Archaeologists have found the shapes and molds of some of the volcano's victims — including this dog — perfectly **preserved** in hardened ash.

Fascinating Fact

The explosion of Mount Pinatubo was one of the most violent volcanic events of the twentieth century. The volcano's eruptions shook the Philippines in June 1991. A total of 19 eruptions took place, spreading so much volcanic ash that the sky remained black for weeks. Mount Pinatubo's disastrous explosions were made worse by the arrival of Typhoon Yuna. This strong tropical storm brought fierce winds and heavy rains. More than one thousand people were killed and over half a million people lost their homes and possessions.

Did you know?

Q. WHAT IS A VOLCANO?

A. A volcano is an opening in Earth's crust through which molten rock and gases erupt.

Q. ARE VOLCANOES JUST MOUNTAINS THAT SOMETIMES EXPLODE?

A. No. The most common type of volcano, a linear volcano, is not even a mountain! It is a long crack in Earth's crust through which lava steadily flows, without violent eruptions. Linear volcanoes are mainly found along the chains of underwater mountains on the ocean floors. A volcano's shape depends on what type of material erupts from the volcano and how that material erupts. When a composite volcano (left) erupts, sometimes only lava slowly oozes out. Other times, the volcano erupts violently, spewing lava, gases, and rock fragments called tephra. The lava and rock from the different eruptions build up in layers around the volcano to form a mountain.

Did you know?

Q. WHAT IS THE DIFFERENCE BETWEEN A HURRICANE AND A TORNADO?

A. A hurricane is a huge, whirling, tropical cyclone, or storm, with winds over 74 miles (119 kilometers) per hour. Hurricanes develop over warm waters in the Atlantic Ocean. (Hurricanes that occur in the western Pacific Ocean are called *typhoons*.) They can be up to 500 miles (800 km) wide, and they often travel long distances before dying out. Tornadoes, on the other hand, usually form over dry land. They cover a smaller area, and they usually travel about 20 miles (32 km) before **diminishing**. Tornadoes, however, can still be very violent, often moving at around 10 to 25 miles (16 to 40 km) per hour and producing winds up to 300 miles (480 km) per hour.

Q. WHAT IS THE EYE OF A STORM?

A. The eye is an area of very low pressure at the center of a hurricane or tornado. Winds swirl around the eye in a **spiraling** motion.

direction of the storm

▲ The United States experiences more tornadoes than any other part of the world. Tornadoes also occur in certain areas of Australia, as well as in Great Britain, China, Canada, France, Italy, Japan, and Russia.

▲ The most devastating typhoon ever recorded took place in November 1970, in Bangladesh. The storm's powerful winds and the huge ocean waves they created killed 200,000 to 300,000 people.

The areas shown in red are where the greatest numbers of hurricanes or typhoons occur each year.

▼ Hurricane Gilbert was one of the strongest hurricanes recorded in the Atlantic Ocean and Caribbean Sea. The storm, which struck in 1988, raked the island of Jamaica and killed a total of 318 people in the United States, Mexico, and Jamaica.

Tornadoes, Hurricanes, ...

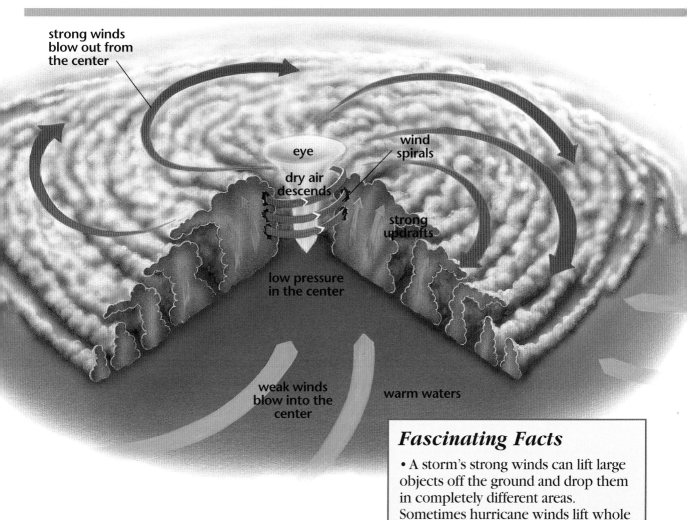

strong winds blow out from the center

eye

wind spirals

dry air descends

strong updrafts

low pressure in the center

weak winds blow into the center

warm waters

Fascinating Facts

• A storm's strong winds can lift large objects off the ground and drop them in completely different areas. Sometimes hurricane winds lift whole schools of fish out of ocean waters and drop them over dry land!

• The energy produced by a hurricane in one day is enough to power all the **industrial** production in the United States for a whole year.

➤ Doppler radar is one of the best tools for predicting tornadoes. This radar can sense when winds are spiraling in clouds. Scientists also can mount the radar on trucks and move it to different areas to check places where tornadoes often occur.

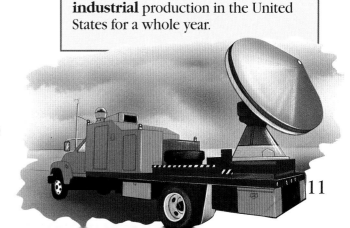

11

... and Other Winds

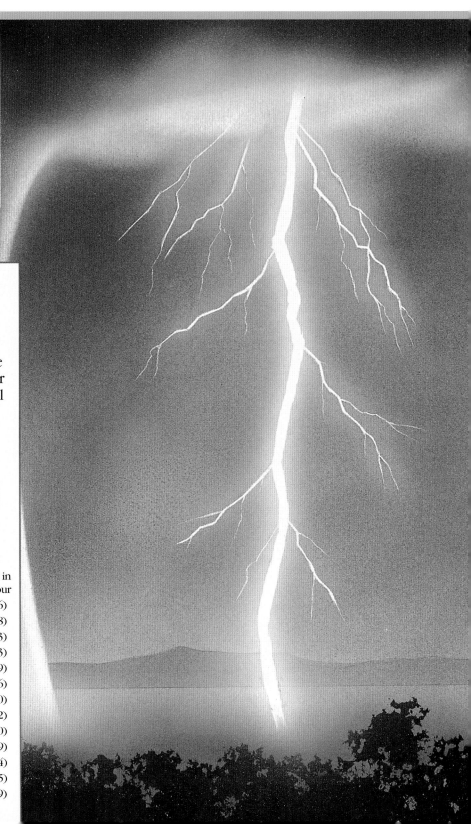

▲ Every day, thunderstorms around the world produce about 100 cloud-to-ground flashes of lightning a second, or 5 million a day.

Fascinating Fact

The Beaufort Wind Force Scale is a range of wind speeds used to classify, or categorize, winds. The scale was invented in 1805 by Sir Francis Beaufort, an admiral in the British navy.

Measurement on Beaufort Scale	Wind Speed in miles (km) per hour
0 Calm	0–1 (0-1.6)
1 Light air	1–3 (1.6-4.8)
2 Light breeze	4-7 (6.4-11.3)
3 Gentle breeze	8-12 (12.9-19.3)
4 Moderate breeze	13-18 (20.9–29)
5 Fresh breeze	19-24 (30.6-38.6)
6 Strong breeze	25-31 (40.2-50)
7 Moderate gale	32-38 (51.5-61.2)
8 Fresh gale	39-46 (62.8-74.0)
9 Strong gale	47-54 (75.6-86.9)
10 Whole gale	55-63 (88.5-101.4)
11 Storm	64-73 (103.0-117.5)
12 Hurricane	over 74 (over 119)

◀ The driest winds blow across desert areas. These winds can reach high speeds, lifting huge amounts of dust and sand that can darken the skies for days. Fine dust swept high up into the **atmosphere** can fall to the ground thousands of miles away. In fact, rains that fall in Europe are sometimes colored red or yellow by particles of sand from the Sahara Desert in Africa.

◀ In summer, a **landspout** sometimes spins over crops, twirling the crops into flattened circles before it dies out.

Fascinating Fact

Heavy storms carrying rain, sleet, or snow often occur when a mass of cold air meets warm, humid air. In March 1993, for example, an enormous mass of cold air moving from the Arctic regions collided with very hot and humid air from the Gulf of Mexico. The Atlantic coast of the United States was blasted by bitter-cold winds of near-hurricane speeds, huge waves, and heavy snowfalls. In just a few days, the weather caused 243 deaths and over $3 billion worth of damage.

During the terrible storm of 1993, even Florida, the "Sunshine State," was covered in snow!

Q. WHAT IS WIND?

A. Wind is the movement of air from one place to another. This movement is often caused by differences in air temperature or air pressure. When two air masses meet, for example, the lighter, warmer air rises and the cooler, **denser** air rushes under it, creating a cool breeze.

Q. WHY DOES WIND BLOW IN FROM LAKES OR OCEANS DURING THE DAY AND TOWARD THEM AT NIGHT?

A. Water in lakes and oceans takes much longer to heat up and cool down than land. Land is quickly heated by the Sun during the day. The air over the land then heats up, rises, and expands. As the air rises, air from over the colder ocean or lake rushes in to fill the space. At night, the land cools off quickly. Now the air over the ocean is warmer and it rises, while cool air rushes out from over the land.

Q. WHAT CAUSES A FOREST FIRE?

A. A natural forest fire can be sparked by lightning or by heat from decomposing, or rotting, plants. Sometimes the heat from lava or ash spewed by volcanoes can trigger a forest fire. The most destructive fires, however, are often started by humans. In some countries, people burn forest areas to make room for growing crops. These fires can spread out of control.

Q. WHAT CAUSES FLOODS?

A. When huge amounts of rain fall in a short period of time, the water levels in rivers rise rapidly until the rivers spill over their banks. Areas around the river are then flooded with water. To stop rivers from flooding, people often build up the river banks to strengthen them or build dams to control the flow of water.

Fires and Floods

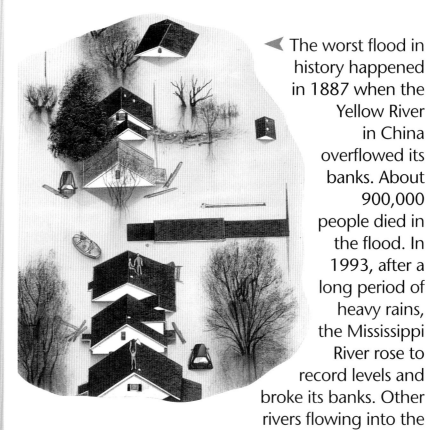

◀ The worst flood in history happened in 1887 when the Yellow River in China overflowed its banks. About 900,000 people died in the flood. In 1993, after a long period of heavy rains, the Mississippi River rose to record levels and broke its banks. Other rivers flowing into the Mississippi also flooded, and more than 38,000 homes were damaged or destroyed.

Fascinating Fact

On June 14, 1960, Kopperl, Texas, experienced an odd, scorching storm. Around sunset, strange clouds spitting bolts of lightning gathered overhead. The temperature climbed to 140° Fahrenheit (60° Celsius), and hot, hurricane-force winds swept through the streets. Plants wilted, and people had difficulty breathing the hot air. No other towns in the area experienced the strange storm. Scientists still do not know what caused it.

Lightning is the most electrifying natural event! One bolt of lightning can carry several hundred million volts of electricity and can spark fires in hot, dry areas.

The flood described in the Bible is one of the most famous floods. According to the Bible, water covered the entire Earth.

Noah (below, far right) built the ark, a large boat, to save Earth's animals from drowning.

One of the most destructive wildfires burned a large part of southeastern Australia in 1983. The fire tore across about 900,000 acres (364,230 hectares) of land. Over 70 people were killed and 8,500 people were left homeless.

Desertification

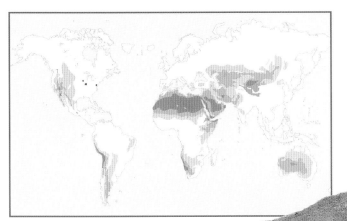

- ■ deserts
- ■ dry areas
- ▓ dry areas that are becoming deserts
- ░ dry areas that are at risk of becoming a desert

➤ More and more areas on Earth are in danger of becoming deserts. Crops cannot be grown in desert conditions, and animals such as sheep and cattle have a hard time surviving, since deserts do not have enough plant life to support these animals.

Fascinating Fact

The Sahara Desert was once a lush, fertile plain, crossed by rivers. Radar photographs show traces of the rivers that once flowed through the region more than 10 million years ago, and signs of more recent waterways also exist. Drawings on cliffs in southern Algeria, in the heart of the Sahara, record how this region slowly became a desert. The earliest drawings are of buffalo, elephants, lions, hippopotamuses, and antelope, as well as of shepherds and hunters. These drawings suggest there once was enough water and plant life in the area to support people and animals. Later drawings, however, depict mainly war carts and camels — the animals, shepherds, and hunters are gone. In fact, in the last 2,000 years, few travelers have passed through the region.

▼ Some countries near the Sahara Desert have problems providing enough food for their people. Unfortunately, the population in these countries is steadily increasing, as the area available to raise crops or animals, such as sheep, is slowly decreasing. The land near the Sahara is becoming less fertile.

Did you know?

Q. WHAT IS DESERTIFICATION?

A. Desertification is the process of fertile land slowly becoming a desert. This process does not just happen near deserts. It can happen anywhere.

Q. WHAT CAUSES DESERTIFICATION?

A. In some places, areas are becoming deserts because of a gradual change in Earth's **climate**. In many places, however, land becomes desertlike because of the actions of humans. People may chop down forests to make room for growing plants or grazing animals, but once the trees are gone, wind and water can quickly **erode** fertile soil. Also, in areas where few plants grow, cattle and sheep can overgraze — they graze so much that they destroy all the plant life. Other causes of desertification include mining and improper farming methods. Scientists believe desertification can be stopped in some areas if people plant trees and use better farming and grazing methods.

Snow and Ice

A. An iceberg is a block of ice that has broken off a glacier or a polar ice floe, a crust of floating ice that forms near the North or South Poles. Carried by the ocean currents and blown by wind, icebergs can travel as many as 8 miles (13 km) a day. They melt as they travel farther from the poles into warmer ocean waters, but they may take many years to melt completely.

Q. WHAT IS AN AVALANCHE?

A. An avalanche is a large mass of snow, ice, rock, or soil that slides down the side of a mountain. Avalanches can be caused when a layer of snow or a mass of rocks is disturbed by wind, earthquakes, a loud noise, or an explosion.

Q. WHAT IS AN ICE AGE?

A. An ice age is a period in Earth's history in which large sheets of ice covered Earth. Huge glaciers spread out from the poles, and many parts of the continents were covered by ice. The average temperature on Earth was much lower than it is today.

◀ The largest icebergs in the world are in the ocean waters near Antarctica. Smaller icebergs are in Arctic waters. Icebergs can be dangerous for ships. Only a small part of an iceberg — about one-seventh — can be seen above the water. Ships that get too close to an iceberg can be damaged by the edges lying beneath the water's surface.

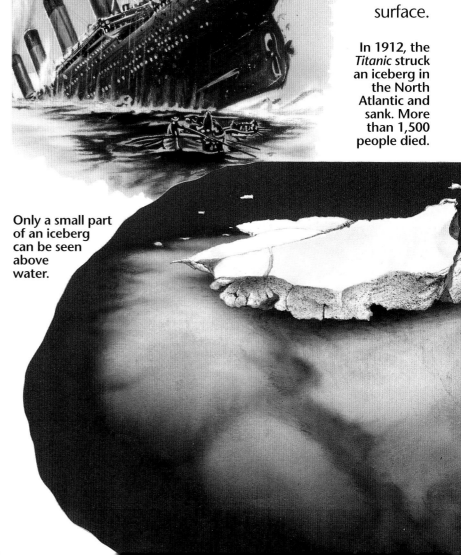

In 1912, the *Titanic* struck an iceberg in the North Atlantic and sank. More than 1,500 people died.

Only a small part of an iceberg can be seen above water.

18

➤ An avalanche that wiped out several towns and villages in Peru in 1970 is one of the worst avalanches in history. An earthquake near Peru's highest peak triggered the avalanche. In just minutes, an immense amount of snow and rock tumbled down the mountain, burying towns in its path. More than 20,000 people were killed.

▲ Mount Washington in New Hampshire has one of the worst climates on Earth. It is located at the point where three major storm tracks meet, and its average yearly temperature is below freezing, or 32° F (0° C). The strongest surface wind speed of 231 miles (372 km) per hour was recorded on Mount Washington in 1934.

Fascinating Fact

From about 1450 to the mid 1900s, temperatures around the world gradually dropped. In Europe, glaciers grew larger and traveled farther down the slopes of mountains, sometimes crushing homes and covering farms. Sea ice choked the North Atlantic, and severe winters in China killed orange groves that had thrived for centuries. Scientists now call this frigid period the Little Ice Age.

Q. WILL THERE BE MORE **MASS EXTINCTIONS** ON EARTH?

A. According to many scientists, the answer is yes. In a survey given by the American Museum of Natural History, seven out of ten **biologists** said they believe the world is currently in the middle of the fastest mass extinction of living things in Earth's history.

Q. IF SO MANY SPECIES OF PLANTS AND ANIMALS EXIST ON EARTH, WHY SHOULD WE WORRY ABOUT A FEW OF THEM DISAPPEARING?

A. The disappearance of even one species can bring unexpected side effects. Galapagos tomato seeds, for instance, have to pass through the **intestines** of a giant turtle in order to grow into plants. If the turtles become **extinct**, the plants will die out as well, taking with them other plants and animals that depend on the tomato plants for survival. Scientists believe that the death of one vegetable species can lead to the extinction of 30 other species that depend on it.

Mass Extinctions

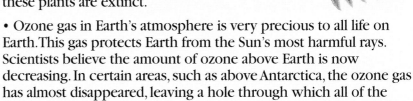

Fascinating Facts

• Animals are not the only living organisms that can experience mass extinction. Plants such as arboreal ferns, club-mosses, and giant horsetails thrived in Earth's forests 290-360 million years ago, but now these plants are extinct.

• Ozone gas in Earth's atmosphere is very precious to all life on Earth. This gas protects Earth from the Sun's most harmful rays. Scientists believe the amount of ozone above Earth is now decreasing. In certain areas, such as above Antarctica, the ozone gas has almost disappeared, leaving a hole through which all of the Sun's rays — including harmful rays — can reach Earth's surface.

▼ The most famous mass extinction is the disappearance of the dinosaurs. About 65 million years ago, a sudden change in Earth's climate killed off about three-fourths of all species on Earth, including these massive creatures.

Fossils are the most important means of studying extinct plant and animal species. Many plant and animal fossils and other types of preserved remains are all that is left of species that are now extinct.

the preserved remains of an extinct Australian mammal

◀ Endangered species are species that face the threat of becoming extinct because their populations are growing smaller. Tigers, rhinoceroses, and condors are some of Earth's many endangered species. Often these animals start to die out when humans use more and more of the animals' **habitats**.

◀ In some areas of the United States and Canada, scientists have recorded a huge increase in the number of **deformities** in amphibians such as frogs (below). These deformities may be occurring naturally, or they may be caused by pollution or by increased exposure to the Sun's ultraviolet rays. Scientists are not yet sure of the causes.

Illnesses

A. Many illnesses are caused by **microorganisms** called pathogens that pass from an **infected** body to a healthy body. Once inside a healthy body, the pathogen reproduces quickly, feeding on whatever **nutrients** it can find. The healthy body becomes weaker and eventually becomes sick.

Q. What is a virus?

A. A virus is a pathogen that lives inside cells. All viruses cause illnesses — some viruses attack animals, others plants, and some people. Viruses are resistant to almost all medicines; the only defense against a virus is through the body's **immune system**.

Q. How do vaccinations work?

A. Doctors put small amounts of a disease-causing pathogen into the body. The body then builds up a defense against the pathogen, so if the pathogen ever enters the body in large amounts, as in an infection, the body can fight it off.

Fascinating Fact

Before the invention of vaccinations, many people died from diseases such as smallpox, tuberculosis, chicken pox, German measles, mumps, and pneumonia, as well as from infected wounds. Through vaccinations, however, people now can fight off these infections. Scientists are always studying new medicines and new ways to fight diseases.

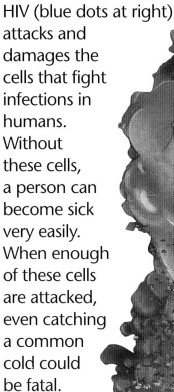 HIV (human immunodeficiency virus) is a virus that causes AIDS, or acquired immunodeficiency syndrome. HIV (blue dots at right) attacks and damages the cells that fight infections in humans. Without these cells, a person can become sick very easily. When enough of these cells are attacked, even catching a common cold could be fatal.

HIV attacks a cell.

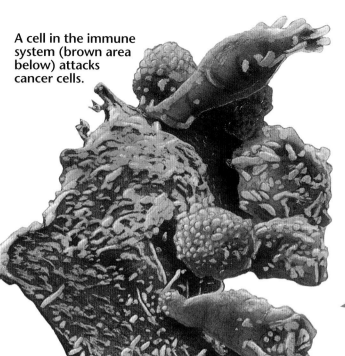

A cell in the immune system (brown area below) attacks cancer cells.

Cancer is one of the most feared illnesses. Cancer is a disease in which cells in the body reproduce and multiply out of control, damaging other healthy cells and interfering with the body's normal processes. Over 100 different types of cancers can affect humans.

A red ribbon is the symbol of the fight against AIDS.

The Ebola virus is one of the deadliest viruses. Seen here magnified more than 13,500 times, the virus has killed more than 80 percent of the people it has infected. It normally has attacked monkeys, however, and only occasionally has infected humans.

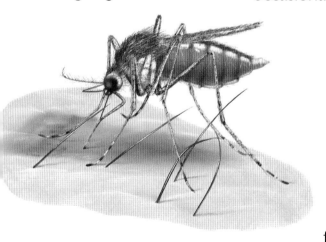

The anopheles mosquito spreads malaria. If one of these mosquitoes feeds on the blood of a person infected with malaria, the mosquito carries the disease and can infect the next person it bites. Malaria is one of the most serious illnesses in the world. According to the World Health Organization, more people die from malaria than from any other **infectious** disease, except tuberculosis.

23

Did you know?

Q. WHAT IS THE BLACK PLAGUE?

A. The Black Plague, or bubonic plague, is a disease that spread through Europe, Asia, and Africa in the 1300s, killing about 50 million people. One-fourth of Europe's population died from the disease.

Q. DOES THE BUBONIC PLAGUE STILL EXIST?

A. Yes, the plague still exists. Today, however, people can receive vaccinations against the plague. New medicines and better **hygiene** also have helped stop the spread of plague and prevented **epidemics**.

Q. WHY IS AIDS SOMETIMES CALLED THE PLAGUE OF THE 21ST CENTURY?

A. Some people consider AIDS similar to the plague because, like the plague, it has spread rapidly and killed millions of people all over the world. People, however, can now be treated when infected with the plague, but scientists have yet to find a cure for AIDS.

◣ A fungus that attacked potato crops in Ireland in 1845 caused one of the worst famines. Potatoes were the main food for many Irish people. The fungus destroyed a year's potato crop and over one million people died of starvation.

Fascinating Fact

In the early 1990s, a disease nicknamed the "Mad Cow Disease" spread through cattle in Great Britain. More than 20 people died after eating meat from infected cows. Almost all of Britain's cattle were destroyed to help stop the disease from spreading.

AIDS, malaria, and tuberculosis are the most widespread infectious diseases. People can receive vaccinations for tuberculosis, but there is no vaccination for malaria or AIDS. Malaria and tuberculosis are not always fatal, but in countries where people do not have the medicine to treat these diseases, many people die from them.

Plagues

The Black Plague is the most famous epidemic. This disease, also called the bubonic plague, is caused by the yersina pestis, a microorganism that usually infects rodents, such as rats. The plague is passed to humans when fleas bite infected rodents and then bite humans. In the mid 1300s many rats roamed the cities, which helped spread the plague.

This scene drawn in the 1300s shows people dying from the Black Plague.

Native American peoples suffered from one of the worst epidemics. When many Europeans first traveled to the Americas, they brought with them several pathogens, including the pathogen that causes smallpox. Native people had never been exposed to these pathogens, so their immune systems had no resistance to them. The smallpox virus killed large numbers of Native Americans. Europeans, on the other hand, had a natural resistance to the disease since it had been in Europe for centuries.

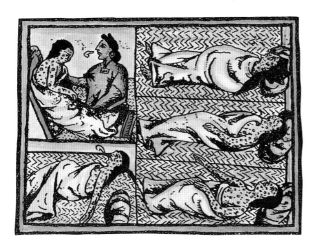

Nature's Oddities

> A hailstone that fell in Coffeyville, Kansas, in 1970 is the largest hailstone on record. It measured 17.5 inches (44 centimeters) around and weighed 1.67 pounds (757 grams). Hail can fall at speeds of over 100 miles (160 km) an hour, severely damaging crops.

> The deadliest tsunami towered 110 feet (33 m) high and swept over 170 miles (274 km) of Japan's coastline on June 15, 1896. The wave destroyed 13,000 homes and left over 22,000 people dead.

▲ A sinkhole in Winter Park, Florida, is one of the largest sinkholes in the world. In just one day in May 1981, the ground under a city block began to sink and gradually 380,000 cubic yards (292,000 cubic m) of earth collapsed, creating a huge hole.

◀ This picture is based on a photograph taken by a Japanese student in Nagano in July 1987. The photograph captured the image of a very rare lightning ball. Scientists still do not know what causes lightning to appear in a ball shape.

Fascinating Fact

Falling meteorites can create huge craters, or pits, in the ground. The largest crater made by a meteorite is in South Africa and measures about 217 miles (350 km) across. One of the largest meteorites ever found landed in Namibia, Africa. It weighs more than 50 tons (45 tonnes) and fell to Earth over 80,000 years ago.

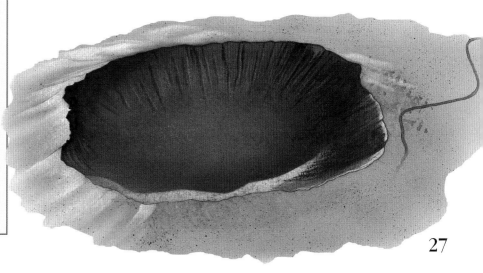

A. Certain gases in Earth's atmosphere act like glass on the roof of a greenhouse — they trap the Sun's heat to keep Earth warm. This natural "greenhouse" effect keeps Earth's average temperature at about 59° F (15° C). Without these gases, Earth would be about 0° F (-18° C)! Humans, however, are increasing the amount of these gases in the atmosphere, causing Earth's temperature to rise. When humans burn fuels such as gas and oil to run cars, heat homes, and power factories, greenhouse gases are given off. Scientists believe Earth's average temperature could rise 2° to 10° F (1° to 6° C) in the next 100 years. A rise of just a few degrees can completely change Earth's climate.

Q. ARE PEOPLE TAKING BETTER CARE OF EARTH?

A. More and more organizations are trying to find ways to solve environmental problems. In every country, more and more people are becoming involved in this work.

Avoidable

Disasters

➤ Several nuclear explosions would send Earth into a "nuclear winter." The dust sucked up into the atmosphere after the explosions would create a "blanket" over Earth, blocking out heat and light from the Sun.

◄ Scientists estimate humans are chopping or burning down rain forests at a rate of 17 million acres (7 million ha) a year, or 33 acres (13 ha) a minute. As the trees disappear, many plant and animal species living in the forests become endangered or even extinct.

▼ Wars have a huge effect on the environment. Chemical plants, oil wells, and nuclear energy sites are often targets for destruction. The bombing of these sites could send harmful chemicals into the atmosphere.

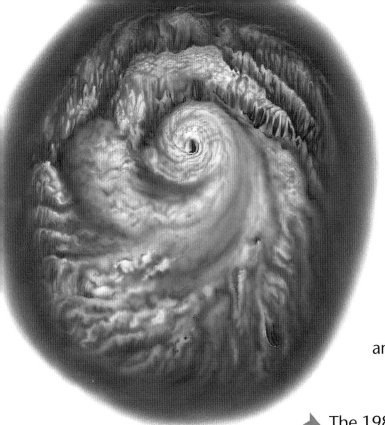

◀ El Niño is a change in the ocean-atmosphere system in the Pacific Ocean. El Niño occurs naturally every four to six years, and its effects can be disastrous. During a severe El Niño, the western part of the Americas suffer powerful rainstorms, flooding, and mudslides, while Southeast Asia and Australia experience forest fires and **drought**.

▲ The 1986 explosion at Chernobyl, a nuclear power plant in Ukraine, is the worst nuclear power plant disaster. The explosion killed 30 people, and many more people have died since the explosion from exposure to **radiation**. After the accident, many people began to oppose the use of nuclear energy.

Fascinating Fact

Is there still enough time to fix Earth's environmental problems? Scientists believe humans can repair some damage to the environment if all the nations of the world work together, because the actions of one country can affect the rest of the world. If one nation pollutes its water supply, for example, that pollution could travel into the water of neighboring countries.

Glossary

atmosphere: all the gases that surround Earth.

biologists: scientists who study living things, including how they function and how they are formed.

catastrophic: disastrous; describing a violent or destructive event.

climate: the average weather conditions over a period of time. A desert, for example, receives very little rain and therefore has a dry climate.

deformities: flaws in body structures, such as an extra leg or a stump in place of a toe.

denser: having molecules, or tiny parts, that are more closely packed together. A rock, for example, is denser than a sponge.

diminishing: weakening; becoming smaller; dying out.

drought: a long period of dry weather without rain or other precipitation.

epidemics: sudden and rapid spreadings of a disease so many people have the disease at one time.

erode: wear down over time.

erupts: bursts forth or explodes from.

extinct: no longer alive, such as when all the animals of one species die out.

fossils: traces or remains of animals or plants from an earlier period of time that are often found in rock.

habitats: places where a plant or animal naturally lives or grows.

hygiene: sanitary practices or conditions that help keep people healthy.

immune system: the system in the human body that protects the body from outside organisms and helps the body fight illnesses.

industrial: relating to the manufacturing or production of goods.

infected: caused to be diseased or unhealthy by introducing a virus or other pathogen.

infectious: able to be spread from one person to another. An infectious disease, for example, passes easily from a sick person to a healthy person.

intestines: the organ in many animals that breaks down or absorbs nutrients.

landspout: a swirling, funnel-shaped cloud that occurs over land and is weaker than a tornado.

mass extinctions: the complete dying out of a large number of plant and/or animal species, such as the mass extinction of dinosaurs.

microorganisms: tiny living things that often can only be seen with the help of a microscope.

molten: melted into a liquid.

nutrients: proteins and other matter an organism needs to survive and grow.

preserved: kept or saved from rotting or decomposing.

radiation: the process of giving off energy in the form of waves or tiny particles.

spiraling: moving in a circular pattern, while gradually moving farther away from the center of the circle. The winds in a tornado spiral around the tornado's center, or eye.

More Books to Read

Avalanche. Nature in Action (series). Stephen Kramer (Carolrhoda Books)

Earthquake. Paul Bennett (Smart Apple Media)

Kids with AIDS. The AIDS Awareness Library (series). Anna Forbes (Powerkids Press)

Natural Disasters (series). Victor Gentle and Janet Perry (Gareth Stevens)

The Nature and Science of Fire. Exploring the Science of Nature (series). Jane Burton and Kim Taylor (Gareth Stevens)

The Science of Weather. Living Science (series). Janice Parker (Gareth Stevens)

Tidal Waves Wash Away Cities and Other Amazing Facts about Stormy Seas. I Didn't Know That (series). Kate Petty (Copper Beech Books)

Volcanoes. Seymour Simon (Morrow, William and Co.)

Wild Weather: Floods! Hello Reader! Science Level 4 (series). Lorraine Jean Hopping (Cartwheel Books)

Videos

All About Earthquakes. Earth Science for Children (series). (Schlessinger)

Heaven's Breath. The Power of the Wind. (New River Media)

National Geographic: Amazing Planet (series). (National Geographic)

Natural Disasters. (DK Publishing)

Web Sites

The Earthquake Shake
www.thetech.org/exhibits_events/online/quakes

Forces of Nature
library.thinkquest.org/C003603/english/index.shtml

Powers of Nature
www.germantown.k12.il.us/html/title.html

Volcano World
volcano.und.nodak.edu/

PBS: In Focus — Floods!
www.pbs.org/newshour/infocus/floods.html

Some web sites stay current longer than others. For further web sites, use a search engine, such as www.yahooligans.com, to locate the following keywords: *avalanche, drought, earthquake, famine, flood, hurricane, natural disasters, plague, tornado, tsunami,* and *volcano.*

Index